Conscious Boundaries

Guided Journal Practices for Setting Limits

Stefanie C. Barthmare

gatekeeper press
Columbus, Ohio

Conscious Boundaries: Guided Journal Practices for Setting Limits

Published by Gatekeeper Press
2167 Stringtown Rd, Suite 109
Columbus, OH 43123-2989
www.GatekeeperPress.com

Library of Congress Control Number: 2022941973

ISBN (paperback): 9781662930058

There is a difference between setting a boundary and knowing your limits. When you are not clear about your limits it is hard to set consistent boundaries with others. You may notice feelings like overwhelm, frustration, annoyance, and impatience when you are not honoring your limits. Practice acting with agency. Make a list of things you can say that will help you hold your ground when you have reached your limit. Write about what it feels like to say things like this out loud: "I have to decline. That day won't work for me," or "Thank you for thinking of me, but I am afraid I can't make that work."

"Quantum science suggests the existence of many possible futures for each moment of our lives. Each future lies in a state of rest until it is awakened by choices made in the present."
—Gregg Braden

What is your body trying to tell you when you feel things like: Tightness in your chest? Rapid heart rate? Excessive fatigue? Irritability? What do you do when you get these sensations? How intense do these bodily sensations have to become before you listen or make changes? What distractions mute the alarm systems in your body? What things can you start doing to help you tune in to your body's wisdom?

"We need to be present, engaged, in the moment, mindful of all that is going on inside us, grounded, focused, and in the here-and-now. If instead, we are in denial, unwilling to confront, closed, shut down, numb, retreating, refusing to feel, protesting, or refusing to accept, then no real grieving can be done." —Martha Stark

People-pleasing is a form of self-abandonment. There may have been a time in your life when it was not safe to speak your truth and accommodating the other was a much safer path. Is this still true? Is accommodating the other person's request more important than attending to your own experience now? Do you feel happy to meet the other's need? What are you hoping to get in return?

"Lost myself trying to please everyone, now I'm losing everyone else trying to find myself." —Nitya Prakash

What price do you pay when you overextend yourself (physically, emotionally, or spiritually)? What price do you pay when you say yes when you mean no? What price does the other person pay when you say yes, and you mean no? What would you risk if you said no more often?

"If you want to live a life of joy and fulfillment, you have to find the courage to break those agreements that are fear-based and claim your personal power." —Don Miguel Ruiz

How do you think others see you? Is that how you want them to see you? Is there more you want others to know about you that you are too frightened to express? What do you fear will happen if you are more open about what you think and feel? What other parts of you long to be seen?

"Nothing in life is to be feared, it is only to be understood. Now is the time to understand more, so that we may fear less."
—Marie Curie

What do you secretly want from others that you believe you will get if you accommodate requests or demands for your time, energy, and attention without any overt or implied request for reciprocity? Do you want more time and attention from others than you ask for? When you don't ask for what you really want, how do you show up in the relationship?

"You have to decide what your highest priorities are and have the courage—pleasantly, smilingly, nonapologetically, to say 'no' to other things. And the way you do that is by having a bigger 'yes' burning inside." —Stephen Covey

How quickly do you bear your heart and soul? What gets in the way of moving slowly and building safety and trust before bringing someone in close? In the pursuit of love, belonging, and acceptance, do you ignore your intuitive alarms and later feel vulnerable or as if the other person has all the control?

"Being able to feel safe with other people is probably the single most important aspect of mental health; safe connections are fundamental to meaningful and satisfying lives."
—Bessel A. van der Kolk

Your attention is your most precious resource. How do you give it away? Who do you do this with? What makes you do this over and over again? When you look to someone else for validation of your worth and you don't get it, how do you feel afterward?

"Stop looking outside for scraps of pleasure or fulfillment, for validation, security, or love—you have a treasure within that is infinitely greater than anything the world can offer."
—Eckhart Tolle

Do you hear your body speaking to you? What does it say to you? Do you listen to your body's signals when you feel hungry? Tired? Lonely? Bored? Are any of these feelings triggers for self-harming behavior? Describe the cycle. You know what it looks like.

"When one is pretending, the entire body revolts." —Anaïs Nin

What specific things have you done lately to avoid conflict? How have you overly accommodated others, but told yourself that it was better to just comply because you don't want to fight? What price do you pay when you give in? Do you later regret it? What would an act of courage and self-advocacy look like today? This month? During the next holiday season?

"Courage is grace under pressure." —Ernest Hemingway

What does it feel like in your body to delay responding to a request? What feelings, stories, or judgments do you think others will have about you when you do not immediately say yes to a request? When someone asks you for something over the next few days, can you pause before saying yes or no? Write down three ways you can delay giving a reply that feels diplomatic and safe. Practice them with someone before you feel put on the spot again.

"Move out of your comfort zone. You can only grow if you are willing to feel awkward and uncomfortable when you try something new." —Brian Tracy

What does it feel like to wait? What feelings arise when you do not get an answer right away? Can you sit with your own discomfort when you don't know if you will get what you want from someone? Make a list of ways you can hold your anxiety when you are uncertain of the outcome.

"Do not worry that your life is turning upside down. How do you know the side you are used to is better than the one to come?" —Rumi

What does choosing yourself mean? What do you risk if you choose your needs over someone else's needs in the present situation you are facing? What is the reward if you choose yourself? How will others react? Does choosing yourself make you vulnerable to criticism or judgment?

"What if each time you experienced an emotion, you acknowledged it, accepted it, and became curious about its message for you instead of trying to make it go away or make it last longer? Imagine how this could change your life. Imagine how heard, loved, and honored you would feel if you really listened to yourself." —Vironika Tugaleva

What can you do in your life right now to practice making yourself a priority? What does it feel like when you do things that are in your best interest? What do others around you do/ say when you take care of yourself first? Is there someone you hope will make you a priority so that you do not have to take responsibility for doing it yourself?

"A life truly lived constantly burns away veils of illusion, burns away what is no longer relevant, gradually reveals our essence, until, at last, we are strong enough to stand in our naked truth." —Marion Woodman

How often do you reach a state of overwhelm before you know you have gone over your limit? What other emotions are tangled up in the experience of being overwhelmed? Is this overwhelm trying to help you find your limit? What can you do to slow down, show up, and start fresh in this situation?

"Trauma can be prevented more easily than it can be healed."
—Peter Levine

What thoughts are running through your head? Are you caught in a loop? Have you become addicted to thinking about this situation in ways that are unproductive? Write about the loop as a way to get it out of your head. Turn the page and leave it for today.

"You are not broken. You are breaking through." —Alex Myles

You are not your thoughts; you are not your interpretations. You can discipline yourself to be free from destructive thinking patterns. You can set internal boundaries for yourself and take back your power. Start now. Write down a few words or a mantra you can repeat to yourself when you get caught in a negative spiral or destructive interpretation of a situation beyond your control. Come back to this mantra repeatedly when the thought arises.

"To free us from the expectations of others, to give us back to ourselves—there lies the great, singular power of self-respect."
—Joan Didion

What are you afraid will happen if you say no? Do you feel brave enough today to practice saying no when you are not willing or able to do something? Make a list of three things you can confidently say no to today, even if it feels painful, unfamiliar or hard.

"Honesty is often very hard. The truth is often painful. But the freedom it can bring is worth the trying." —Fred Rogers

What is the payoff for you when you give people what they want? What image or perception of yourself are you trying to maintain by being so accommodating? Are you aware of the price that you pay when you people-please?

"We must not allow other people's limited perceptions to define us." —Virginia Satir

How often do you commit to plans when you actually need downtime? How do you show up when you are over-committed and exhausted? Does staying busy and saying yes distract you from anything that you need to be doing to take care of yourself at a deeper level? Make a list of things you have been avoiding. Now get to work. You can do this.

"When we stop expecting another to give us wholeness, we can take the risk of finding our own sense of wholeness; we can discover and encourage our own complementary energies, the inner masculine and feminine aspects of ourselves." —Jill Mellick

Being perfectly attuned to others is impossible. Mistakes happen. Feelings get hurt as a result of misunderstandings and misattunement. What do you do when you have hurt someone's feelings (intentionally or by mistake)? What do you say to others when you notice their feelings have been hurt? How do you initiate a repair cycle? What thoughts and feelings make it hard to extend an apology to the other?

"A mistake that makes you humble is much better than an achievement that makes you arrogant." —Sheikh Hamza Yusuf

How do you react when someone has hurt your feelings? Has this happened recently? How about when someone gets angry with you? How do you respond? Has this happened recently? What happens when others are not able to take responsibility for being hurtful or angry with you? How do you handle it? Is sarcasm one of your go-to defenses? What does the sarcasm protect you from?

"A lot of times we don't feel able to express what is uncomfortable or painful in a vulnerable way, so we do it with sarcasm, avoidance, or some complaint." —Stefanie C. Barthmare

What messages did you get as a child about privacy? Did others respect your need to be alone? Were you allowed to close the bathroom or bedroom door when you needed to be by yourself? Were you allowed to have things that belonged only to you? Were you pressured to share your belongings? How do you feel now about sharing? How do you protect yourself, your time, and your stuff as an adult?

"The things that women reclaim are often their own oice, their own values, their imaginagion, their clairvoyance, their stories, their ancient memories. If we go for the deeper, and the darker, and the less known we will touch the bones."
—Clarissa Pinkola Estes

Do you feel comfortable expressing your opinions about food, restaurant choices, or social outings? How comfortable are you if your preferences are different from those around you? Any new behavior must be practiced repeatedly before it becomes familiar and comfortable. Make a list of things you like and dislike. Start to speak of your preferences. Notice how others respond and see what happens.

"The most important part of any new habit is getting started—not just the first time, but each time." —James Clear

What parts of your personality are a facade or a false self? In what ways have these parts been constructed to please others? How do you think these false parts developed? Why do you allow others to believe that you are one way when really, at your core, you are not that way at all?

"In order to realize our true self, we must be willing to live without being dependent upon the opinion of others." —Bruce Lee

How comfortable are you with getting feedback from others? Does everything you hear sound like criticism? Can you tell when you are activated by another person's evaluation of you or your work? What can you do to expand your interpretation of how others are experiencing you? Their observations may have a tiny grain of truth, or they may not be accurate at all. When you are regulated, you will know the difference.

"Regulate, relate, and reason." —Bruce Perry

How do you feel when someone says no to you? How do you behave when you feel this way? How would you like others to respond to you when they have reached their limit and cannot meet your need? How comfortable are you when someone cannot give you an answer right away?

"Be more responsive, less reactive." —Diane Poole Heller

What role do you play in letting people take advantage of you? No matter how small the percentage, what is the role you play in how it happens? What are you willing and able to do to begin to interrupt this pattern so you feel more empowered and in charge of your experiences?

"Nothing ever goes away until it has taught us what we need to know." —Pema Chödrön

What three feelings best describe you today? What messages do these feelings bring you about your body's needs today? What three words best describe your energy level today? What do you typically do when you have this level of energy? Do you let your feelings and your energy level influence how much you do in a day? How often do you connect with your internal experience and let it influence your activity? How often do you override these internal signals?

"Embrace the glorious mess that you are." —Elizabeth Gilbert

What does taking responsibility for yourself and standing up for your needs mean to you? How can you do a better job of holding yourself accountable for getting your needs met and speaking your truth? What three things could you do this week to stand up for yourself? Take action and write about it.

"I not only have the right to stand up for myself, but I have the responsibility. I can't ask somebody else to stand up for me if I won't stand up for myself." —Maya Angelou

Author Bio

Stefanie C. Barthmare, M.Ed., LPC-S, has been a licensed psychotherapist for over 20 years. She holds degrees from both The University of Texas and The University of Houston. Stefanie formerly worked at Houston Methodist Hospital where she counseled patients in groups and individually and authored a monthly newsletter, Staying Connected, for over ten years. Stefanie currently works in private practice with couples and individuals seeking deeper insight and stronger, more intimate relationships. She developed this collection of self-discovery journals for individuals desiring a deeper exploration of their inner world.

Follow Stefanie on Instagram @distinctivepractice.

Made in United States
Orlando, FL
09 November 2022

24374308R00043